T0380972

The Works of
Martin Vincent Paul

MARTIN VINCENT PAUL

AuthorHouse™ UK
1663 Liberty Drive
Bloomington, IN 47403 USA
www.authorhouse.co.uk
Phone: 0800 047 8203 (Domestic TFN)
+44 1908 723714 (International)

Because of the dynamic nature of the Internet, any web addresses or links contained in this book may have changed
since publication and may no longer be valid. The views expressed in this work are solely those of the author and do not
necessarily reflect the views of the publisher, and the publisher hereby disclaims any responsibility for them.

Any people depicted in stock imagery provided by Getty Images are models,
and such images are being used for illustrative purposes only.
Certain stock imagery © Getty Images.

This book is printed on acid-free paper.

ISBN: 978-1-7283-9757-3 (sc)
ISBN: 978-1-7283-9756-6 (e)

Print information available on the last page.

Published by AuthorHouse 01/31/2020

authorHOUSE®

Dedication

I would like to dedicate this book to my loving grandmother Anastasia (Ma) Paul and my aunt Eliza Beauty John, the two most influential people in my life. Your love and support is the reason I am the person that I am today.

Heartfelt thanks to my aunt Winifred John, uncles Highland, Happyman, Mrs Jean and Otice John.

Uncle Babs and Cline Paul your love and support has been priceless.

To the Paul and John family, you are forever in my heart. Thank you for your continued support

Contents

1. You paved a way

Because of you I am standing proud and firm today
In my head there is so many things that I want to say
For I am truly happy that you grew us up the right way

All that you taught us gave us so much pride
Your instruction to us would always be our guide
It was great to know that you're always on our side

You brought us up proud so we can take a stand
When we were down and needed you, you gave a helping hand
In this confusion only someone like you can truly understand

Forever in your debt we are all in a better place
Bringing a better today for a tomorrow that we can face
You have made a difference in our life's you are truly our ace
What I wouldn't give to once again be in your space

I have spoken my peace and my words are clear
And now the time has come when I must switch to another gear
Now the whole world must know why in my heart I hold your words so dear

2. Beautiful things that we share

When I think of all the beautiful things that we share
It makes me so happy to know that, you really care
I will always be standing by your side so please be aware
I adore you my darling I must, I cannot imagine any less, I won't dare

My feelings for you are real I hope my words can explain
Am so very happy to be in your presence once again
I won't let this opportunity to be in love with you go in vain
When you were gone, my heart was broken and I was left in pain

3. I love you more and more every day

I love you more and more every day
My love for you is real and here to stay
I love you more than my words can ever say
If ever you need me I will be by your side without delay

You will always have a special place in my heart
I had these feelings for you right from the start
Finding you again makes me happy, I look real smart
I will be there for you in your corner no matter what

4. I enjoy when we talk

Just to let you know how much I enjoy when we talk
Looking forward to us being together I will enjoy that walk
I'm forever so impressed with your intellect you're so smart
Despite all the circumstances that separate us and keep us apart
You were always so graceful I was amazed right from the start

I want to thank you for rising beyond my expectations
It's nice to see you didn't let the distance set any limitations
Life pulls us in different direction but you move forward without reservation

These words I write I hope you can understand
That it may help me to develop into a very good man
Sometimes you have to let your conscience be your guide
My words can be deep at times but comes from my heart deep inside
They express the real me in and out my true feeling this I cannot hide

5. I want you to believe

I want you to believe in the words coming from my mouth
My beautiful life with you is what I am talking about
Our life together is amazing and beautiful without any doubt
You in my life to stay because you I don't ever want to live without
Just believe in me forever and the words coming from my mouth
I will be there standing by your side each and every day of every month

Despite your discomfort and pain you looked so beautiful tonight
For you are unique in every way I thank God for showing me the light
Every step you take you give your best with all your might
You look so beautiful, especially when you are in my sight

6. I will still love you when things ain't right

I will still love you when things ain't right
Keep loving you always even when we fight
I won't forget you when you're out of my sight
When we are together our future looks bright

I won't ever be a fool and let you get away
I will treasure your present in my life every day
But, my actions will speak more than my words today

7. When the road gets rough

When the road gets rough, I will be there to stand by your side
I will be there when your burden get heavy
I will be the one in whom you can confide
These words I speak is real my feelings I cannot hide
I will be there to support you my arms are open wide

You are an amazing person you lift me up and set my heart on fire
My emotions are high you start me thinking about my heart desire
My emotions moving in all directions like a thread hanging on a wire

8. Don't want to live my life without you

Don't want to live my life without you by my side as no one can ever take your place
You will always be in my heart, you're part of my life, you hold that crucial space
How wonderful my life would be to wake up every morning to your beautiful face

My love for you is forever
Don't want to leave you never
Together we can battle the stormy weather
As I value all our time that we spent together
One thing is for sure my life with you in it is so much better

I am happy for you, especially for the things I cannot change
Learning to hold on regardless to how things get strange
Rest assure our happiness is close, it is within our range

9. Queen in my castle

You are the queen in my castle
My genie in my bottle
You are my worldly treasure
My love for you has no measure
Captain steering my lonely ship
You're my champagne for me to sip

You are my world with no end
My angel and my best friend
A greater angle God could not send
I will be waiting always around the bend

I want the world to know our story
Now that I have won your love my victory
Looking forward to being with you in a hurry
My love for you is forever you don't have to worry

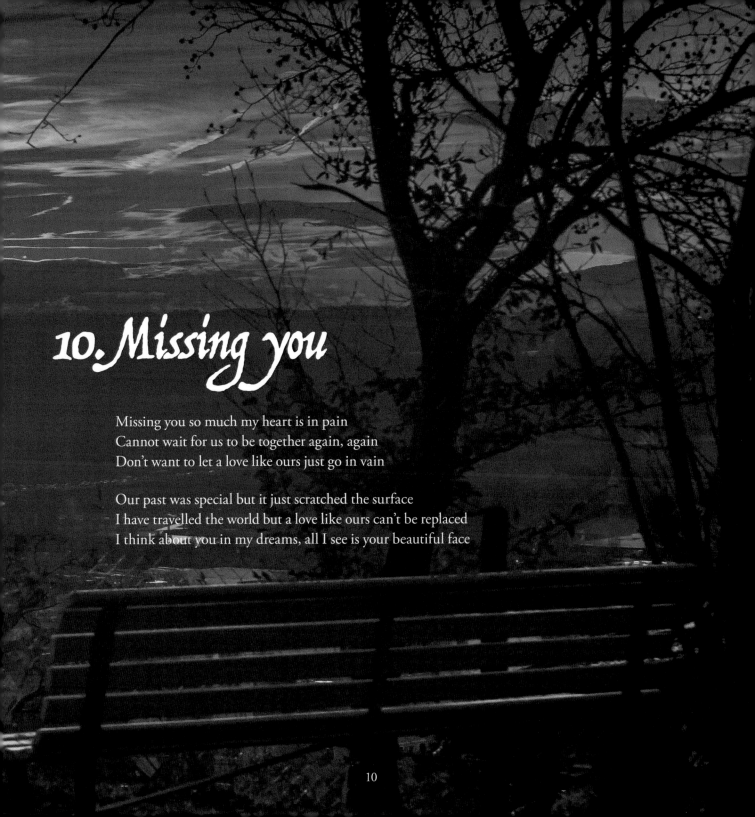

10. Missing you

Missing you so much my heart is in pain
Cannot wait for us to be together again, again
Don't want to let a love like ours just go in vain

Our past was special but it just scratched the surface
I have travelled the world but a love like ours can't be replaced
I think about you in my dreams, all I see is your beautiful face

11. It's amazing

It's amazing how everything within you just glow
Our relationship is forever as it grows and grows
We have no choice but to let our love just flow
Accepting your love as much as the heart will allow
Believing in a higher being wherever God leads we will follow

I have accepted our faith and let our love move just as slow
Every day that goes by I want you more and more
well I never knew real love existed like this before
You have given me a life sentence to love you forever more
You help me to forget about all my sorrows
You help me to look forward to our tomorrows

12. People are people

People are people wherever you go, why not treat them all the same
When things go wrong we have to bind ourselves together without no shame
No one person should have to stand by themselves to ever take the blame
We all need each other that is a fact of our existence in life it is not a game

Looking at how things may change from day to day
Some of us just hoping that some love will come our way
But for me I will be standing in the gap for my brother I am here to stay

13. Looking back

Looking back it was you that I wanted right from the start
The negative things that were spoken just broke my heart
Now that that you back in my arms, nothing can tear us apart

I will cherish you and all our special moments
Forsaking all the people negative comments
Holding on all the love and the sentiments

All day communication just talking on the phone
One thing is for sure I will never leave you alone
By your side is where I will be after all is said and done
These feelings are real so strong I feel it in my bones

14. So far away

It is so hard for me that you are so far away
I miss you dearly each and every single day
But it is certain that my love for you is here to stay

My life without seems so unjust
Call on a higher being if you must
But in me you must put your trust

A greater match of you and me they have never been So much passion and love the world have never seen
People may try but they cannot separate or get in between

15. How can I live without you

When I go to sleep at night, getting a good night's rest is my biggest fight
just so you would know in my dreams you are the biggest highlight
In your absence I would toss and turn without you I just turn and turn
When you are far away I always feel that in my heart one day you will return

When you are away what happens to you is really a great cause for my concern
Asking myself how can I live without your face around me in my sight
You are the one that keeps me up in my darkest hour you're my shining light
Now I hope you can understand without you my future don't look so bright

I search and look all over a better partner I could not find
Didn't see it before because maybe I was just too blind
As I grow older I realize you are truly one of a kind
The sacrifice am willing to make I really don't mind
Now we can look forward to our future living all difficulties behind

16. Sunshine in my life

You're the sunshine in my life my bright light
Making me happy and alive day and night
Now that you in my life my future looks so bright

In the past when things went wrong I must take the blame
But I can promise you this time around things will not be the same
I am giving you all my love for that and I won't be a shame

I want to be with you, look in your eyes day and night keeping you close
Because your love for me is a cure for my heart just need a greater dose
When we are together don't want to ever let you out of my sight
Just want to correct where I went wrong and make things right

17. My shining star

In my life every day you are my shining star
You make me complete whether you're near or far
I need you on my side to compete with this love and war

I can tell you now I love you beyond any measure
Your memories in my heart I truly really treasure
You are everything that I want my destiny my future
When we are together we standing on solid structure
Thinking of my life without you in it will be pure torture

18. your smile

Your smile shines within you ever so bright
As your spirit creates this magnificent light
Combine together it just makes me happy day and night
Your energy takes us all to a new level of a different height

Makes me want to keep you close forever within my sight
This what we share is so special, I won't ever give up without a fight

You in my life takes me to a place I have never been
You have shown me things that I have never seen
What we are sharing is so special no one can separate or come in between

19. You set my heart on fire

You set my heart on fire like a burning flame
To lose what we shared together would be a shame
What a glorious day it will be to hear you say my name
Because without you by my side my life will not be the same
These things I am feeling for you my love comes from deep inside
The time has come when I have to let you know in you I must confide

20. No better feeling

Being with you there is no better feeling
When I found you I hit the highest ceiling
You opened my heart to love you and I was willing

With you is where my heart belongs
Giving my love to you I cannot go wrong
For loving you is what keep me forever young

I have looked all over and a love like ours I can never find
I wake up happy every day because you are always on my mind
You are so amazing truly very special you are really one of a kind

21. Always fighting to declare my worth

Always fighting to declare my worth
Life without you is so painful I can feel the hurt
As I examine my life on this earth

You are one of the reasons for my existence
The love we shared gives me courage and resilience
Understanding together we make a big difference

What we have together no one can eliminate
In everything we do we must have an associate
Someone to love you and whom you can appreciate

In you I put my trust along with my values and faith
Giving thanks that you will forever be my mate
You have my best desire I gave you my ultimate
How wonderful to finally live with someone that understand
How good it is to have that special someone and a helping hand

22. Feeling sad

Feeling sad to know all the things that happened I was wrong
I want to make it up to you let me know if am coming on too strong
Let me keep loving you the way a man should love his woman

Whatever your desire your wish will always be my command
Supporting you always next to you my dear is where I will stand
The only wish I have is you will keep letting me be your only man

23. He gives nothing but love

I know the God I serve
He gives us nothing but his love
He delivered us more times than we deserve
I will be forever grateful to the God I serve
Fighting hard for my place in heaven to be reserve
His spirit alive comes from a place far up and above

He is almighty more powerful than anyone that came before
When his light shines on you don't have to depend on anyone anymore
These things I am feeling for him now I can no longer ignore

Now am living my life in his most desirable grace
That is how I know tomorrow problems I can honestly face
My father your love for me I can never replace
When my mind is blank you are always there to fill
the empty space
That is why your love for me I am ready to embrace

24. The things I say to you

These things I say to you for you my words are true
Understand for only you holds the keys to my future
If you think your replaceable you don't have a clue
for we have to stay
To have you back in my life would be my pleasure
When my heart is broken only you have the cure

You are the one that change my reality when am feeling blue
Hence I am feeling so close to you now as we bond together as glue
Things I feel for you inside for you my heart is pure
You are worth more to me than gold, you are my personal treasure

Without you by my side my heart is so broken
Judge me not by my words, but by my actions taken
Never before has fewer words have ever been spoken
We were so happy once, sometimes I wonder have you forgotten

It is you that I want by my side, this I know I am certain
Regardless to what happens between us, I won't complain
That's why I would keep coming back again and again

25. Right now my love

Right now my love for you my dear is so strong
By my side no doubt is where you belong
With me by your side you can never be wrong

In you I put all of my values, my trust and my pride
The time has come my dear when you must decide
Because for you right now my love my arms are open wide

These feelings for you my dear I cannot ignore
Days go days come I want to be with you more and more
These feelings for you I have never felt before

My love for you should not come as a surprise
So please listen to my simple words as I have advised
As a man grows older in life he may become very, very wise

26. Living my life without you

Living my life without you makes me unhappy and sad
Moving forward not knowing where we are is really bad
Remembering you and me together and what we had
To have one more chance to be with you I would so glad

The memories of you my love is forever on my mind
You are truly magnificent person, really one of a kind
The wonderful person that you are inside and out

A more beautiful person I could not find
I did not recognize your place in my life, I'm sorry I was so blind
It's so good to know that no one can separate us now that our resources are combined

27. Miles apart

Even though we are miles and miles apart
You hold a very special place in my heart
From the very first time we met, I felt this way right from the start

Even if you are miles away the warm feeling of you is with me to stay
Most of all, most important I pray that you keep safe each and every day
I am so very happy that you are back in my life once again
The joy that you have brought into my life, I must one day explain
My life was so empty without you, but now is not the time to complain

It is up to us to keep our relationship going I promise not to let a love like ours fail
All my feelings are focused on you, like am locked up in your mental jail
Just waiting for you to one day free my emotions and to stand my bail
I can just imagine me and you together in the ocean of love as we sail

28. The distance between us

The distance between us makes my love for you grows
When it's pouring rain my love for you just flows
When the sun shines my love for you just glows
With my emotions running high, I have to take it slow
Whatever your plans I'll be standing with you to follow

In my arms my love is where I want you to stay
Your love is more than money can ever buy
This is why my love I want you to make me your guy

29. Expectations

Expectations are high, but not higher than I can deliver
You are always on my mind, you will be with me forever
Your joyous spirit will be with me, I will forget you never

I am not happy when you are out of my life without a trace
Now that you are here, your smile, your beautiful eyes, gentle touch, I am ready to embrace
I will swim the deepest oceans, climb the highest mountains to put a smile on your face
Memories of you and me together in love can never be replaced

30. Happy beyond imagination

You make me happy beyond my expectations
You have taken me place beyond my imaginations
I feel that you are one of God's greatest creations
You support me always and gladly offer solutions

Nothing can separate us, because of our special bond
I will always love you forever and beyond
I will climb the highest mountain just to be with you
My faith in you is unwavering just as the sky is blue

I will love you beyond any measure, that's my choice
Because when I think of the joys of you my spirit rejoice
I can never forget you or leave your memories behind
You are so special, never have I met someone so kind

31. Your absence

In your absence I realized my love for you just grew
I couldn't pinpoint the time when things changed, but I can't imagine you being with someone new

I tried to explain it all in different ways, but words are just too few
My thoughts of you in my head is left dangling as the wind blew
Just don't want to ever think of you with someone new

You brought my inner thoughts to reality, my life now have substance
I bring to you love like I've never had before, you have my assurance
In you I put all my trust, your kind heart certify my existence

32. My loyalty

One thing is for sure, my loyalty for you runs deep
All that I have my dear is for you my love is yours forever to keep
You are forever in my thoughts, I think of you every night before I go to sleep
In your absence I am glad you are not around to see me weep

In your absence I see your face at every turn
I may have travelled the world, but cannot survive without you, that I've learnt
Trying to protect myself from your love, I don't want to get burned
At the end of the day, I'll be waiting for the day when you will return
So now that my message to you is clear, I am grateful for the day you were born

33. So proud

I am so happy you made me so proud today
I search myself for words more than I can say
If ever you need me I will be by your side without delay

My happy feeling for you I cannot hide
Stirring my emotions for you on the inside
Opportunities are endless the world is open wide
I am so happy to be bless with you in my life I must confide

Words cannot explain all the things I want to say
For you brought me so much joy on this special day
I just hope things will keep going your way
Like a card game in your life we all have our part to play

34. You are marvelous

You are marvelous and incredible always inspiring me to give my best
I can be all I can be with your endorsement as I am separated from the rest
Meeting all the world expectations with love excellent and dedication passing all the test
Protecting myself from life disappointment covering my heart with a bullet proof vest
I am so excited with life new prospective I can hear my heart beating in my chest

I am traveling all over the world with you from East to West
Traveling down a rocky road with you am not afraid to take a ride
One thing is for sure my life is an open book from you there is nothing to hide
Because I know to be with you is clear to me by your rules I must abide

35. Be confident

Rest assured you are the one that holds all my love
Be confident in you and me whatever problems arises we can rise above
One day soon you and me together will fly away like a dove

For it is your love my dear I have been waiting for so long
Hoping and praying that between us nothing will ever go wrong
I am truly certain that with you is where my heart belongs

36. To be with you

To be with you I will travel to the moon
In my absence you must know I will be back in your arms soon
So keep your eyes on the prize I will be back before the clock hits noon

To be with you I am willing to pay whatever price
Just to get back what we lost I will make the sacrifice
Together we can give our relationship the attention it deserves and proper service
You are the one I value the most, I always seek your input and personal advice

37. Original love

In closing I must let you know, that my love for you is original there is no other copy
Putting you up on a pedestal, you will always be my private and personal trophy
We would live our lives in a world where there is happiness forever that will be our philosophy
So this will be the final chapter to our happy life and magnificent biography

As we learned to accept our life and the things, we cannot change
When we commit to discuss the issues, we must stay engaged
We have to be glad we have each other and always stay within our range
In closing, you are the original there is no other copy

38. My queen

Only you can interpret my love and what it really mean no one can come between
The truth be told In my world you are beautiful and exceptional my only queen
I Search all over Could not find anyone to match your character where ever I have been
It is indeed remarkable you remain the most beautiful person I have ever seen

So I want to make myself clear to you as these things in my heart unfolds
My words may reflect these happy inner feeling is for you my dear to have and to hold
Today as as I write I want my words to speak of my love for you if I may be so bold

After all is said and done clearly in my mind for you I have planted a seed
In my infinite wisdom and understanding where others may have failed I hope to succeed
As my dreams conclude for me one day soon for your love one day I will hold the only deed
I have come to realize my hunger for your love only you can one day could feed

39. I must declare.

For you my love I must declare
I would love you forever without fear
To give you any less I won't dare
So keep my words close to your heart ♥
And know that I really care

Keeping in mind that my words to you are so real
Coming from my heart it is sign with my personal seal
If you search me all over only then will my heart reveal
How my love for is so real.

40. True Love is to Embrace

No one has the right to make anyone feel disgraced
because true love is really for the whole world to embrace
Sometimes people disappear out of your life without a trace
To avoid the hard things in life that we sometime have to face

It is important as a society we don't drop the ball
That it is necessary to stand for humanity even if we fall
Don't take long to reconnect as the world awaits your call
With the majority on our side we can feel like we ten feet tall

41. Speak to Injustice

Give love to the people that speak to the injustice
They sacrifice themselves but how many people notice
They defend the unjust
Stand with them now we must
And now we must give them our trust

Society tells you to be quiet do as you are told
But common sense is not common you have to know when to fold
Reality is people are still mentally brought and sold
It happens in our society because the people responsible behave bold
Hard to believe that men will betray their own brothers for something call gold
That being said to advance in our society you have to put your conscience on hold

42. Knowledge is Power

Knowledge is something the hold world should acquire
Being educated in our society should be everyone desire
Because to have certificates and diploma is what the future require
Finally An educated man or woman someday can set the world on fire

So now we have to set examples for everyone to follow
Stop living a life where you appears to be shallow

To live your life the way you want and not behind someone shadow
Keep positive ideas going so one day someone will want to barrow

43. You bring me joy

The thought of you brings a smile to my face
I just wish we could all live in the same place
You bring me joy when ever we are together
You must know Your memories stay with me for ever

When I am with you you give so much
You reach places no one else has ever touch
You throw so.love at me so I can catch
That no one else in the world can ever match
Now we are all on display for the hold world to watch

I will keep loving you where ever you are
I will keep loving you when you are near or far

Printed in the United States
By Bookmasters